the early
1920s
to the mid
1930s

MODERN ERAS UNCOVERED

From Speakeasies to Stalinism

Pat Levy

www.raintreepublishers.co.uk

Visit our website to find out more information about **Raintree** books.

To order:
☎ Phone 44 (0) 1865 888113
🖷 Send a fax to 44 (0) 1865 314091
🖳 Visit the Raintree Bookshop at **www.raintreepublishers.co.uk** to browse our catalogue and order online.

First published in Great Britain by Raintree, Halley Court, Jordan Hill, Oxford, OX2 8EJ, part of Harcourt Education.
Raintree is a registered trademark of Harcourt Education Ltd.

Editorial: Melanie Copland, Tameika Martin, and Lucy Beevor
Design: Michelle Lisseter and Bridge Creatives Services Ltd
Picture Research: Mica Brancic and Ginny Stroud-Lewis
Production: Duncan Gilbert

Originated by Chroma Graphics (Overseas) Pte.Ltd
Printed and bound in China by South China Printing Company

ISBN 1 844 43951 8 (hardback)
10 09 08 07 06
10 9 8 7 6 5 4 3 2 1

British Library Cataloguing in Publication Data
Levy, Patricia
From Speakeasies to Stalinism. – (Modern Eras Uncovered)
909.8'22
A full catalogue record for this book is available from the British Library.

Acknowledgements
Corbis/Bettmann pp. 5, 13, 20, 21, 28, 34, 35, 36, 42; Corbis/Francis G Mayer p. 14; Corbis/Hulton-Deutsch Collection pp. 7, 16, 25, 40, 46; Corbis/Sean Sexton Collection p. 22; Getty p. 49; Getty Images/Hulton Archive pp. 4, 6, 10, 11, 12, 17, 23, 24, 26, 27, 29, 30, 32, 33, 37, 39, 41, 44, 48; Getty Images/Time Life Pictures pp. 18, 38, 45; Mary Evans Picture Library/Meledin Collection p. 31; Illustrated London News p. 55; Novosti Press Agency p. 47; The Advertising Archives Ltd pp. 8, 19; The Art Archive/Musée National d'Art Moderne Paris/Dagli Orti (A) © Salvador Dali, Gala-Salvador Dali/Foundation, DACS, London 2004 p. 15.

Cover photograph (top) reproduced with permission of Corbis/Bettman, and poster (bottom) reproduced with permission of Novosti Photo Library.

BROTHER CAN YOU SPARE A DIME?
Words and Music by E. Y. Harburg and Jay Gorney
© 1932 Harms Inc, USA
Chappell Music Ltd, London W6 8BS
Reproduced by permission of International Music Publications Ltd.
All Rights Reserved.

CONTENTS

Any words appearing in the text in bold, **like this**, are explained in the glossary.

The First World War ended in 1918. This war had caused more death and destruction than any other war in history. As a result of the war, **empires** collapsed and there was a **revolution** in Russia. The war had created political problems in other countries that would eventually lead to the Second World War.

In the 1920s, no one knew what was to come. All over Europe and the United States people decided to put the past behind them and look to the future. They talked about the First World War as "the war to end all wars" and did not imagine that something as dreadful as that would ever happen again.

This is a view of a crowded Manhattan street during the "roaring twenties," New York, United States.

A new way of life

For women especially, the war had made life very different. Many women went out to work, to do the jobs that the men fighting in the war had left. Some wealthy young women, called flappers, started going out to dance halls and clubs to enjoy the new American **jazz** music. In the United States, many people broke the law by drinking alcohol, in clubs called **speakeasies**. There were new cinemas, where audiences watched their favourite stars like Rudolph Valentino, or Charlie Chaplin. Because of the new ideas and excitement that was around, this period was called the "roaring twenties".

A whole new world

In science, important new discoveries and technologies were about to change people's lives. New drugs such as **penicillin** would help fight **tuberculosis** and other deadly diseases. The new technology of aeroplane flight meant wealthy people would soon be flying around the world. Cars drove down city streets between huge skyscrapers. Electric light, running water, and vacuum cleaners made the lives of wealthy people easier than ever before. World news was heard on new, wireless radios in people's homes. These radios also gave people music, stories, comic shows, and science programmes.

The Arts

Artists were creating new ways of expressing themselves. Writers such as James Joyce and Virginia Woolf wrote about the inner thoughts of their characters in ways that were very new. Painters such as Salvador Dali tried to show how the human mind works in their paintings.

American influences

In the 1920s, American **culture** began to have more and more influence around the world, especially in Europe. Much of the new technology for making cinema and cars came from the United States. The United States was also very wealthy – it had enough money to help the UK out of the debt that the First World War had left it in.

The Wall Street Crash of 1929 in the United States brought the **economies** of the world tumbling down with it. It caused huge unemployment. It also led to **dictators**, such as Hitler, getting into power by offering simple solutions to their country's problems. Concerned with its own huge problems, in 1929, the United States turned its back on Europe to sort itself out. By the time the United States started to get involved with Europe again, the problems in Europe had led to another world war.

A flapper describes herself

"If you judge by appearances, I suppose I am a flapper. I am the right age. I wear bobbed hair, the sign of a flapper. (And, oh, what a comfort it is!) I powder my nose. I wear fringed skirts, bright-coloured sweaters and scarfs, and low-heeled shoes. I adore to dance. I spend a large amount of time in automobiles. I attend dances, and proms, and ball-games, and crew races, and other affairs at men's colleges."

(FROM A FLAPPER'S APPEAL TO PARENTS BY ELLEN WELLES PAGE)

Young women, known as flappers, perform the Charleston, a dance made popular in the mid 1920s.

Wages rose in the UK in the 1920s. More people were able to afford gadgets for their homes and leisure activities such as trips to the seaside. People went to the cinema to see silent films or spent the evenings listening to the first public broadcasts on their radios. The wealthy had cars to tour the countryside, telephones to talk to their friends, and electricity to light their parties. The poor stayed poor, but could afford the occasional day trip.

The Jazz Age

In New Orleans, Chicago, and New York in the United States, a new kind of music was emerging. It developed from the chants that black slaves had sung while they worked. Bands such as Louis Armstrong's Hot Fives, Duke Ellington's Cotton Club Orchestra, and Jelly Roll Morton's Red Hot Peppers filled clubs. A female black singer called Bessie Smith sang a slow kind of music that came to be called the Blues. Young white people became interested in this black music and it found its way on to the new radio stations. White bands like the New Orleans Rhythm Kings began to copy the sound.

American blues singer Bessie Smith in 1923.

Dance marathons

During the 1920s dance marathons began in some cities in the United States. Couples competed to see who could stay on the dance floor for the longest time, before the judges knocked them off. Dance marathons sometimes went on for months. There was big prize money and professional dancers would travel around from one marathon to another. Alice Elinor, an American journalist, described some dancers recovering during a rest period. The women taking part were exhausted and lay half unconscious at the side of the dance floor. One girl was moaning in pain:

"Bending over her is a man, her trainer, who massages her swollen feet. Beside her, another girl is lying. Flies crawl across her closed eyes and buzz against her chin."

(FROM *SEATTLE POST-INTELLIGENCER*, 8 AUGUST 1928)

New dances such as the Charleston swept through the dance clubs of the world. These were lively and fast dances where people kicked up their heels like never before. Bands of professional musicians made a living by touring cities where dances were held in public ballrooms. Ordinary people could buy music to play on their **gramophones** – old record players. In the United States and UK wealthy young people, known in the UK as "Bright Young Things," behaved outrageously compared to the strict standards of the time. The women wore revealing clothes, smoked, drank alcohol, and stayed out all night. In Germany, **cabaret** became very popular. Berlin, the capital, became the centre of a new culture of enjoyment.

Couples compete in a marathon dance event on a cruise ship sailing between Venice and Los Angeles in the United States, 1923.

The new woman

When the First World War came to an end, men who had been away fighting returned to their homes and jobs in the United States and Europe. The women who had done their jobs now had to leave the factories and offices and go back to being housewives. It was not so easy for women's lives to go back to the way they had been before the war. During the years of the war women had taken over their husband's role as head of the household. They had managed the family's money and had experienced independence like never before. Even their clothes had had to change, because they were doing jobs that could not be done in the tight **corsets** and large skirts of the early 20th century. Skirts were now lightweight and shorter, and many women began to cut their hair short. This was partly for fashion, but also because it was more convenient.

This advertisement shows the new, comfortable female fashion designs of the 1920s.

The new look

New technology had helped women to achieve this new, modern look. Rayon, a man-made fabric, had been invented. It was cheap, lightweight and easily washed. It could be made into stockings. Before rayon, stockings could only be made from silk, which was very expensive. The zip was invented in Chicago, United States, in 1893. It soon spread to Europe and became an essential part of the new clothes. By 1926, an average woman's outfit weighed one tenth of what it weighed at the end of the 19th century.

Along with the new lightweight clothes and the short hair came another new look for women. The ideal figure for how a woman in the late 19th century should look had been a large chest, thin waist, and wide hips. This "hourglass" shape was achieved by wearing huge and uncomfortable corsets. These were laced at the back and pulled in at the waist tightly so that every woman, no matter what her natural shape was, could achieve the hourglass figure. The new fashionable shape of the 1920s was slim, flat-chested, and with no visible waistline. The trendy young women, called "flappers", wore tubular dresses with fringes that flapped as they danced the new dances. Some of the party dresses that the flappers wore were backless, which shocked older members of society.

Barbara Cartland remembers

Barbara Cartland, a British novelist, remembered the time when she and her friends cut off their long hair into **shingles**, a short hairstyle with a fringe across the face. She said that she and her friends had copied the new style to be different. They did not want to be like the war widows who were dressed in huge black dresses, with long hair and hourglass shaped clothes. She said:

"To shingle was to cut loose from being just a mother or a wife. It was an anti-sentimental symbol, not an anti-feminine one."

They didn't want to be like their mothers. The new fashion meant that they could be free of all the sadness of the war.

(FROM *WE DANCED ALL NIGHT* BY BARBARA CARTLAND)

Going to the cinema

In the late 19th century, scientists had invented very simple ways of making moving pictures. By the 1920s, hundreds of short, silent films were being made each year. Cinemas opened up in every town and they employed musicians to play while the silent films were running. All over the United States and Europe people began to go to the cinema once or twice every week. Movie actors such as Rudolph Valentino, Gloria Swanson, Mack Sennet, Harold Lloyd, and Buster Keaton became famous for their films. Charlie Chaplin became the first internationally famous star. In 1926, Rudolph Valentino died suddenly at the age of 31 and thousands of people visited his body as it lay "in state" in New York.

Italian–American movie actor, Rudolph Valentino, stars in the famous movie adventure *The Son of the Sheik* in 1926.

European cinema

In the UK, the film industry did not have the money to compete with US movies, but in Russia, Germany, and France a different kind of film-making flourished. US movies were adventure stories about cowboys, horror films, historical stories, or comedies. In Europe, film became a new way for artists to express themselves rather than a popular form of entertainment. In Russia film directors were experimenting with new ways of editing film and telling stories. Early movie audiences generally believed everything they saw on film and governments all over the world quickly came to realize that film could be used to encourage people to support the government.

The "talkies"

In 1926, a whole new world of cinema opened up when the first film with sound was made. Musical comedies became very popular. In 1928, Mickey Mouse, created by Walt Disney, was the first animated cartoon with sound. In the United States and Europe, cinema owners rushed to set up sound systems in their theatres. Silent movies became out of date and some silent movie actors suddenly found themselves out of work because their voices did not suit the "talkies."

British-born film star Charlie Chaplin plays his famous "little tramp" character in the 1915 film *The Tramp*.

Charlie Chaplin

Born in England in 1889, Charlie Chaplin was acting and dancing by the age of eight. His childhood was a difficult one after his father died, and his family were often very poor. In 1906, aged seventeen, he found a job in a travelling theatre show and in 1910 went with them to the United States. He decided to stay there and in 1913 was offered a job in the movies in New York. Chaplin invented film characters and his sad figure of the poor, unloved tramp became world famous. By 1915, he was so famous he was allowed to direct his own films and his salary rose to US$1,250 a week in 1915. In 1917, he was offered US$1 million for a series of eight films. He formed his own film company, United Artists, which still exists. Charlie Chaplin is considered to be one of the greatest film-makers of all time.

Speakeasies

Since the late 19th century, many people in the United States had come to believe that alcohol was a cause of crime, poverty, and violence. In 1920, the manufacture, sale, or distribution of alcoholic drinks was banned in the United States. Canada had already banned selling and drinking alcohol a year earlier.

Police officers destroy barrels of alcohol during prohibition in the United States, January 1920.

Prohibition

The law banning alcohol, called **prohibition**, was a popular one because many people believed that alcohol needed to be controlled. The ban, however, was very unsuccessful. There were not enough police to enforce it. The illegal manufacture of alcohol became widespread. Illegal bars known as "speakeasies" emerged and became very popular. People especially enjoyed the idea of spending an evening in a smoky bar with some jazz music in the background and the thrill of knowing there might be a police raid at any moment.

A crime wave

The sale of alcohol was taken over by criminals who became very rich. On every street corner soft drinks saloons had secret back rooms where people who knew the right password could enter. Here, they drank "bootleg" alcohol, transported by night from the West Indies, or from Canada, which had quickly ended its own ban on alcohol. The centre of the illegal alcohol industry was Chicago. Here, gangsters, with the co-operation of some police, judges, and politicians who were paid large sums of money to ignore what was going on, ran a huge crime operation. It extended from trading in alcohol to gambling and **protection rackets**.

An interview with Al Capone

During prohibition the journalist Claud Cockburn interviewed Al Capone. Capone praised the freedom of the US system and said he was proud of his American background and of the early American settlers. "Listen," he said, "don't think that I'm knocking the American system. My rackets," he repeated several times, "are run like American businesses and they're going to stay that way."

(FROM *I CLAUD* BY CLAUD COCKBURN)

Onlookers watch as police remove the bodies of the victims of a gang-related murder in Chicago, United States, 1929.

EXPRE

Gang warfare

In Chicago, rival gangs fought for control of the illegal businesses. During prohibition there were 500 gang-related killings in the city. Al Capone ruled the Chicago gang world for a decade. In 1929, he was responsible for killing seven members of a rival gang in what became known as the St Valentine's Day massacre.

The end of prohibition

By the 1930s, **economic depression** had begun in the United States, and the public and the government believed that the unemployed needed back the jobs that had been lost in the legal brewing and whisky-making factories. People also disliked how the government was limiting their freedom to drink alcohol. A law making alcohol legal again was passed in 1933.

In the UK there were enormous changes going on in science, health, and fashion. The average family had more money to spend during the 1920s, more leisure time, better access to medicine and **birth control**, and a growing awareness of fashion and the arts. In fashionable and wealthy society, a great wave of change swept through traditional culture. Everything from kitchenware to the work of artists and writers was influenced by new ideas in art and science.

Modernism and realism

Modernism was a type of art that started before the First World War and developed fully in the 1920s. Modernism involved a complete change from the fashions, the art, and the ideas of the previous generation. In American art this took the form of **realism**. Realism had developed in the late 19th century, but in the 1920s and 1930s it focused on the grim reality of city life and the **Depression**. American artists such as Edward Hopper and George Bellows painted ordinary people in their everyday lives. Georgia O'Keeffe also rejected traditional styles of painting and chose to paint in an **abstract** way.

This is one of Edward Hopper's famous realist paintings, *Automat*, from 1927.

Surrealism

In Europe in the 1920s a different modern style was growing. In 1924, a French writer called André Breton published a description of a new idea called surrealism. He explained that surrealism, in art and in literature, blurred the boundaries between dreaming and waking. Surrealists were influenced by Sigmund Freud. Freud was a doctor who had developed psychoanalysis – a way of studying people's minds to understand their mental illness. Freud studied people's dreams to find meanings. A French painter called Max Ernst developed a way of painting where he tried to let ideas and images develop without any **conscious** control. A Spanish artist, Salvador Dali, painted very realistic paintings but included visual tricks in his work. In Dali paintings a landscape could also be a face, for example, making them like dreams where reality and fantasy are merged.

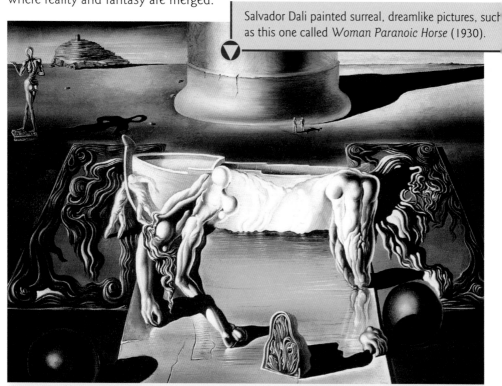

Salvador Dali painted surreal, dreamlike pictures, such as this one called *Woman Paranoic Horse* (1930).

Georgia O'Keeffe

Georgia O'Keeffe was born in 1887 in Wisconsin, United States. She studied and later taught art at colleges and universities. Her early paintings were exhibited in New York City. She soon became famous, with exhibits in galleries all over the United States. Her paintings of the 1920s show ordinary things such as a single flower or a cattle skull, but painted in close up so that they look unusual. She continued to paint for many years and her paintings can still be seen in museums around the United States.

Books and buildings

In the 1920s, modern writers had begun to experiment with new ways of writing. They became interested in how they wrote as well as the story that they wanted to write. For example, one of the most important **modernist** writers, the Irishman James Joyce experimented with a style of writing called "stream of consciousness." In this style he wrote down the thoughts of his characters as they popped into their heads.

In Paris, a woman called Sylvia Beach ran a bookshop and published the work of people like Joyce whose experimental writing could not find a publisher. In London, a group of writers and artists known as the Bloomsbury Group were also finding new ways of expressing themselves. One of these was Virginia Woolf who also used the "stream of consciousness" technique in her novels.

The lost generation

In the United States, modernist writers such as Ernest Hemingway and William Faulkner wrote about the grim reality of life and the horrors of the First World War. Ellen Glasgow wrote about the southern states of the United States, while F. Scott Fitzgerald wrote about sophisticated wealthy Americans. Lots of young American writers moved to Europe for inspiration and one of them, Gertrude Stein, gave them a name – the "lost generation."

The novelist Virginia Woolf, pictured here in 1902 at the age of twenty, was a central figure in the Bloomsbury Group.

Architecture

After the First World War architects began to want simple designs and materials to work with. Many were inspired by a German, Walter Gropius, who set up a school of architecture called Bauhaus. Its idea was that the appearance of a building should be decided by its use, and not by fashion or style. Modernist buildings looked very plain, with flat roofs and concrete walls.

The first skyscrapers

In the United States, by the end of the 19th century, architects had designed high rise buildings using steel frames as support. Skyscrapers became possible in 1889 after the electric lift was invented in the mid 1880s. In 1930, the Chrysler building was constructed in New York and became the world's tallest building at 320 metres (1,050 feet). Modernist designs made the building both tall and striking. In 1931, the Empire State building in New York topped the record at a height of 381 metres (1,250 feet).

This view of the Empire State building in 1932 shows the top tier still under construction.

James Joyce

Born in 1882, James Joyce grew up in poverty in Dublin, Ireland. He was a talented student and was given scholarships to the best school in Dublin. He went on to university, but quickly decided that his life in Dublin was too restrictive. His early short stories were too harsh and unusual for Dublin publishers. By 1920, Joyce was living in Paris and, in 1922, his novel Ulysses was published. Reactions to the novel, which was very inventive as well as being outspoken about sex, were extreme. Copies were seized and destroyed on government orders in both the United States and UK.

New designs and fashions

To match the new buildings, a new style of interior design emerged called Art Deco, named after an art exhibition in Paris in 1925 called *Arts Décoratifs*. It was abstract and sharp edged, and it was inspired by ancient civilizations such as the Aztecs and Egyptians. The typical patterns adopted by Art Deco – chevrons, sunbursts, pyramids, and lightning flashes – were used in thousands of buildings. In the United States, classic examples of this style are the interior of Radio City Music Hall and the decoration on the Chrysler Building in New York.

UK archaeologist Howard Carter examines the patterned coffin of the Egyptian Pharoah Tutankhamen, which he discovered in the Valley of the Kings, Luxor, Egypt in 1922. Graphic Egyptian patterns, such as these, inspired the new Art Deco styles of the 1920s.

A democratic art form

When Art Deco was first developed it was only available to the very wealthy, in elegant buildings and on beautiful furniture. It was around this time that new materials such as Bakelite (an early form of plastic) were being widely used. As Art Deco became more popular, more and more everyday items, such as wireless sets, ornaments for the fireplace, or armchairs for the parlour, were made in the Art Deco style.

Furniture

Many designers were inventing ways of making beautiful, cheap furniture. In 1930 in Finland, a designer called Alvar Aalto started making curved wooden furniture from thin sheets of plywood. In Germany, Marcel Breuer began designing similar furniture, but this time made out of tubular steel.

Light

The rooms in new modernist buildings were big open spaces with very little clutter in them and big windows. The skyscrapers and modern buildings of the cities with their electric power were as brightly lit at night as they were by day. Designers created light sculptures from glass and **Perspex** panels. In 1932, the **anglepoise** lamp was invented and put into **mass production**.

The anglepoise lamp

One of the most successful household objects to be created during the Art Deco period was the anglepoise lamp. Most people today have a version of this lamp either at home or at work. Based on the human arm, the lamp is jointed and can be moved into any angle to focus light in a particular place. The original 1932 edition of the anglepoise lamp was made from painted steel with a Bakelite shade and looked very much like the modern ones.

Kitchens

Most people still ran their homes without things like washing machines or vacuum cleaners. For those who could afford luxuries, there were new electric or gas stoves, which were stylish in design and **enamelled** for easy cleaning. New crockery and pots and pans were Art Deco in style. Refrigerators were just as beautifully designed and were also enamelled for ease of cleaning.

This 1920s advertisement for silver-plated cutlery shows how designers used the Art Deco style to make everyday items beautiful.

THE QUEST FOR BEAUTY GOES ON

To the accomplished hostess, the beauty of her Silverware must be as irreproachable as her dinner gown. She requires of design the assurance she finds in a Paris model. Community Plate gives her this assurance—in the Deauville or any other of its six distinguished creations. And with it is the added distinction of Patine the Community finish that gives the Silverware luminous loveliness. You may have a Community Service for Six for as little as $36.50—for Eight, $48.00; a three-piece matching Tea Set for $40.00—wherever fine Silver is sold.

TUDOR PLATE Silverware is also made and guaranteed by the makers of Community Plate.

The DEAUVILLE Design

COMMUNITY PLATE
LEADERSHIP IN DESIGN AUTHORITY

Science and technology

Frank Conrad sits with the first broadcast radio set in his garage in Wilkenburg, Pennsylvania, United States, March 1924.

Many of the inventions and new designs in the 1920s and 1930s were due to scientific breakthroughs. Other new technology made radio, cinema, and the earliest television sets possible. In 1928, John Logie Baird, a Scotsman, first transmitted a picture across the Atlantic from the UK to the United States. In the United States in 1928, the first television broadcast was made by the television station WGY. The first regular television broadcast in Britain was made by the British Broadcasting Corporation (BBC) in 1936.

Flight

In flight technology there were enormous changes taking place. Aeroplanes had been used in the First World War, but many pilots were unemployed after the war. Some European countries recognized the potential of air travel, and governments set up national airlines. By 1928, airships, called Zeppelins after their inventor, were carrying passengers across the Atlantic from Europe to both North and South America. In 1927, Charles Lindbergh became the first man to fly solo across the Atlantic from New York to Paris. In 1932, the American Amelia Earhart became the first woman to fly solo across the Atlantic.

Astronomy and physics

Great advances were made in astronomy during the 1920s. In 1924, the American astronomer Edwin Hubble worked out that the universe was made up of many galaxies and not just the Milky Way. In 1917, Albert Einstein had suggested that the universe was expanding, and in 1921, he received the Nobel Prize for his work. This led Georges Lemaître, a Belgian, to suggest that the universe began with a gigantic explosion – a "big bang." The expanding universe, Lemaître suggested, was due to the material moving away from the centre of the explosion just as when something is blown up on Earth. Besides being interesting to scientists, this new information about the universe led to a popular interest in the stars and science fiction.

In 1932, Amelia Earhart became the first woman to fly a plane solo across the Atlantic.

Medicine

In 1921, two Canadian scientists discovered a substance called **insulin**, and so were able to treat people suffering from **diabetes**. The most important medical discovery of the time was in 1928 when Alexander Fleming accidentally discovered a mould that could kill certain types of bacteria. He developed this to make the first **antibiotic** – called penicillin – which helped to save the lives of millions of people.

Simple but unreliable forms of birth control had been available long before the 1920s. But in 1921 Margaret Sanger founded the American Birth Control League in the United States. This organization promoted the idea that clinics give advice and effective **contraceptives** to the women who visit them.

POLITICAL REBELLION

The UK came out of the First World War a very different country from the one that had entered it. Women had put aside their demands for the vote while the war was raging, but now they felt they had earned more rights. Men returning from the war felt they were owed better working conditions than they had previously experienced. In Ireland and India, both parts of the **British Empire**, **nationalists** were demanding freedom.

Ireland demands independence

In 1919, an Irish nationalist party called Sinn Fein (Ourselves Alone) began a war of **independence** against Britain. They set up their own government and launched a **guerrilla war**. In response, the British government introduced laws that allowed them to arrest and imprison people without charging them with any offence. It also gave the army powers to tell ordinary citizens what to do. This increased support for the nationalist guerrillas, especially when the British army used violence against civilians.

A negotiated settlement

In 1921, the British Prime Minister Lloyd George offered a peace settlement that would allow 26 of the 32 Irish counties to become independent while 6 counties in the north of Ireland would remain part of the UK. The majority of the population in the 6 counties was **Protestant** and wanted to remain part of the UK. Irish nationalists did not want to split Ireland into two, but eventually agreed. The **treaty** they signed created a Protestant-dominated region in the north of the country called Northern Ireland.

The Irish soldier Michael Collins signed the 1921 treaty that created the Republic of Ireland and Northern Ireland.

Civil war

The treaty caused serious disagreements among Irish nationalists, and in 1922, a **civil war** broke out. One group accepted the treaty as they thought it would lead to full independence in the future. The other group rejected the treaty. The group that accepted the treaty won the civil war, but there were still disagreements. Northern Ireland remained a problem because all nationalists agreed that it should be part of a united Ireland.

Crowds gather to view the bombed-out ruins in O'Connell Street, Dublin, during the Irish Civil War, July 1922.

The Croke Park killings

On 20 November 1920, Irish nationalist guerrillas killed twelve British army officers in Dublin, some of them in front of their families. Later the same day British troops surrounded Dublin's football stadium, Croke Park. A football match was taking place and hundreds of people were trapped inside. Whether someone in the crowd fired on the troops or whether the troops imagined that they did will never be known, but eleven people in the crowd and one of the football players were shot by the British army. Many more people were wounded. In Ireland and around the world people blamed the British army for taking revenge for the earlier killings through these murders.

India demands independence

By 1918, the UK had ruled India for nearly 200 years. After the First World War, when over a million Indian men had fought for the British, many Indians started demanding independence. In 1919, at a public meeting in Amritsar in northern India, British troops fired on the crowd and killed 379 people. This led to a peaceful protest movement led by Gandhi.

Gandhi's philosophy

Gandhi believed that non-violence could be used to make the British give India her independence. He called on people in India to refuse to buy any British goods, take part in elections, or pay any taxes. Gandhi was an extremely popular and well-loved leader. All over India people did what he asked and thousands were arrested and imprisoned. Gandhi himself was arrested in 1922 and sentenced to six years in prison. He was arrested and sent to prison many times over the next decade and each time he began a **hunger strike**. This forced the British authorities to release him.

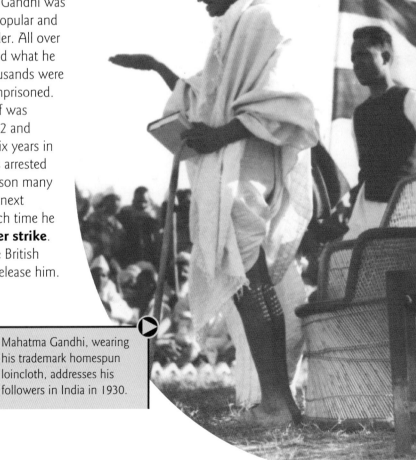

Mahatma Gandhi, wearing his trademark homespun loincloth, addresses his followers in India in 1930.

The salt tax

In 1930, still trying to force the British to give India its independence, Gandhi again called on people to refuse to pay taxes – this time it was the salt tax. This was a very unfair tax since even the poorest people in India had to find money to pay for salt. People need the sodium in salt for their bodies to function properly. A year after the **boycott** began, 60,000 people were in prison.

Gandhi walks in the Salt March of 1930, which was a protest against the unfair salt tax in India.

Salt tax boycott

During the salt tax boycott, hundreds of men and women went to a salt deposit and walked slowly and unarmed towards it. Webb Miller, an American journalist, witnessed what happened next. As each group of citizens walked towards the salt deposit local policemen hit them with clubs. As each group fell, another group replaced them and were also knocked down. Miller later went to the first aid camp where the injured were being treated and saw hundreds lying there. Two people had been killed.

The untouchables

Gandhi had other concerns besides Indian independence. Indian Hindu society was made up of castes or social groups. Each caste would have been given different voting rights in an independent India. While in prison in 1932, Gandhi began a hunger strike to draw attention to the treatment of India's lowest caste, the untouchables.

Gandhi had always tried to keep all the religious groups in India united against Britain. In the early years this had worked, but by the 1930s Muslim groups in India had begun to demand a separate country from the Hindus. India did not become independent until after the Second World War, and after independence there were many deaths as Muslim and Hindu communities fought one another.

General Strike in the UK

After the First World War most countries had out of date and underdeveloped industries. In the UK, the coal mining industry in particular was very run-down. In the early 1920s, mine owners, who needed money to improve their mines at a time when coal prices were very low, decided to cut miners' wages and increase their working hours.

The lock out

In 1926, when talks broke down between the miners' **trade union** and the pit owners, a **strike** was called by the miners. In response, the pit owners locked up the mines and refused to let the miners back in. In support of the miners, the Trades Union Congress (TUC), which represented all the unions in the UK, called for a general strike of all workers across the country.

This British street is crowded with strikers during the General Strike, January 1926.

The General Strike

For 9 days, in May 1926, 3 million workers stayed away from work. There were no bus services, trains, trams, newspapers, or building works, and no power was generated except for emergency use. Striking workers stood outside the gates to their factories and offices and refused to allow people or transport in or out. The one exception was food, which they allowed to be transported to shops.

Around the country people who refused to join the strike and people who disagreed with the strikers' actions drove buses or trains. They were known as strike-breakers. Armed troops were posted at government offices, docks, and other important sites to stop strikers from causing any trouble with the strike-breakers. They had orders to fire on the strikers if it became necessary. Fortunately this never happened, but as the days went by, the strike-breakers got fed up with driving buses and stoking steam engines and it became obvious that the strike was working.

The strike ends

After 9 days, the TUC met the mine owners who offered a slightly better deal for the miners. The TUC ordered the miners to accept it. They called off the strike and everyone went back to work – except the miners. They refused to accept the new terms and stayed on strike until November. By then, however, their children were malnourished and winter was approaching, so they gave in. Their wages were decreased, their working hours were lengthened, and they went back to work.

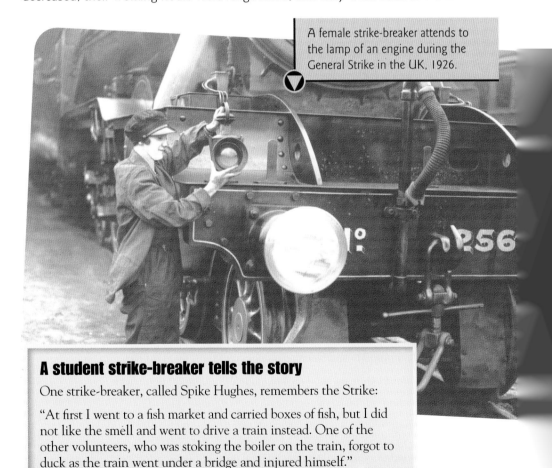

A female strike-breaker attends to the lamp of an engine during the General Strike in the UK, 1926.

A student strike-breaker tells the story

One strike-breaker, called Spike Hughes, remembers the Strike:

"At first I went to a fish market and carried boxes of fish, but I did not like the smell and went to drive a train instead. One of the other volunteers, who was stoking the boiler on the train, forgot to duck as the train went under a bridge and injured himself."

(FROM OPENING BARS BY SPIKE HUGHES)

Fascism in Italy

Italy came out of the First World War with economic and political problems. Factories were producing more goods than people could buy, and there were thousands of returning troops who had no jobs to go back to. The country was also divided between those who had supported the war and those who were against it.

Fascism

Into this political trouble stepped various groups with highly **patriotic**, nationalist feelings. They went around the country breaking up strikes and attacking **socialist** organizations. The leader of one of these groups was Benito Mussolini. He put into words the ideals that these nationalist groups were fighting for and called it **fascism**.

The Italian dictator, Benito Mussolini, addresses a huge crowd from his balcony at Pistoia, Italy, 26 May 1930.

Mussolini believed that political policies were less important than strong leadership. He saw war as a way of getting what the country needed, by making people more patriotic and willing to make sacrifices for their country.

Unlike the UK, France, and Germany, Italy did not have much of an empire, but Mussolini promised to turn the Mediterranean region and North Africa into a new Roman Empire.

Mussolini's rise to power

In May 1922, discontented workers in Italy called a general strike. Mussolini saw this as his opportunity. By this time his fascist party had supporters all over Italy and he announced that if the government did not stop the strike then the fascists would.

Although Mussolini's party held only a tiny proportion of the seats in the Italian **parliament**, the King asked Mussolini to take over as prime minister. Mussolini demanded the powers of a dictator and was given them. Across Italy, fascist groups attacked socialists and trade unions, and newspapers were **censored**.

Mussolini's policies

Mussolini set about organizing the economy, passing laws that would increase industrial and agricultural production. He told other Western leaders that Italy offered no threat to them and he was warmly welcomed by world political leaders. They hoped that Italy would help keep the peace between Germany and France.

The great dictator

The son of a blacksmith, Benito Mussolini was a bright, good looking, young man with piercing eyes. He became a **communist** and earned his living as a journalist. During the First World War he suddenly changed all his ideas and became a believer in dictatorship. Mussolini loved to address the crowds at rallies where he and his supporters dressed up in striking black uniforms. He was a great speaker and could influence the crowds that came to watch him. His speeches had lots of arm waving and shouting. Often the things that he said were wrong, but people loved him so they cheered him on.

▲ Supporters of the Italian dictator, known as "Black Shirts," march past Mussolini in Italy, October 1935.

China and Russia

In the 1920s, political **rebellions** were not only breaking out in Europe. They were also taking place in China and Russia, two huge countries whose empires had collapsed earlier – the Chinese empire had been overthrown in 1911, the Russian in 1917. The question now was, what sort of governments would emerge?

Rule of the warlords

After 1911, the government in China came to depend on several military dictators, called warlords, who ruled different regions of the country. These warlords fought amongst themselves for the control of **territory**. At the same time, European powers, such as the UK, continued to enjoy making profits from their trading posts in China.

Mao Zedong

In the early 1920s, two new groups called for freedom from the warlords. Chiang Kai-Shek became the leader of one of the groups and he tried to destroy the other group, who were communists. One young communist, Mao Zedong, led his group on a 6,000-mile (9,600-kilometre) trek in order to escape from Chiang Kai-Shek. This was in 1934, and the trek became known as the Long March. Although Chiang Kai-Shek claimed to represent China, he did little to help the millions of poor peasants and workers. Mao Zedong was determined to keep his rebellion going and to help the poor.

The leader of the Chinese Communist Party, Mao Zedong, during the Long March of 1934.

Rebellion in Russia

In 1917, there had been a communist revolution in Russia. A civil war then raged between the communists and the parties opposed to communism. By 1921, the war was over and the communists had complete power. Lenin's government took complete control of all the businesses in the country, including the distribution of food from the countryside. This eventually led to a terrible famine in 1921, when 6 million people died. Lenin began to behave like a dictator and communists who had once supported him now rebelled.

The sailors of Kronstadt

Kronstadt was an important naval base near Petrograd (St Petersburg) and the sailors had been keen supporters of the 1917 revolution. But, in 1921, 16,000 sailors rose in **mutiny**. They thought the revolution was being betrayed and the government was becoming a dictatorship. They were ordered to surrender by Lenin's government, and when they refused, the army moved in and crushed the rebellion.

Soviet government forces (on horseback) take control of Kronstadt on 17 March 1921, ending the sailors' rebellion.

The sailors' demands

In 1921, the sailors of Kronstadt published a list of their demands, which included:

- to hold new elections immediately
- to give freedom of speech and press to workers and **peasants**, to **anarchists** and socialists
- to free all political prisoners of socialist parties
- to equalize the food rations of all working people
- to give peasants full freedom of action in regard to the land, and the right to keep cattle, on condition that the peasants manage with their own work without employing hired labour.

(FROM *THE ANARCHISTS IN THE RUSSIAN REVOLUTION* EDITED BY PAUL AVRICH)

At the end of the First World War, the UK found itself in debt. By 1921, there was a serious economic depression, with almost a quarter of the workforce unemployed. The UK's old industries – textiles, shipbuilding, and mining – were badly run-down and were being overtaken by better producers such as Japan. The UK also felt the effects of the economic problems in countries such as Germany, which could no longer afford to buy UK goods.

German economic collapse

Germany had huge war fines to pay to the **Allies** as a result of losing the First World War. By the early 1920s, Germany was also suffering from severe **inflation**. Prices rose and wages had to rise with them. By 1923, Germany was unable to make its payments, so France and Belgium invaded the Ruhr (Germany's main industrial area) and tried to take over its industries.

Hyperinflation

German workers and factory owners began refusing to co-operate with the occupying troops. The German government supported the workers and began paying them **social security** payments. In order to do this it had to print huge amounts of money. The value of German money fell against all other currencies and prices began to rise faster than wages could be increased. The price of a loaf of bread rose in one day from 20,000 marks to 5 million marks. People carried their wages home in wheelbarrows. On 15 November 1923 the mark (the German currency) collapsed completely. Its exchange rate with the US dollar was 4.2 trillion marks to 1 dollar. People who had carefully saved up all their lives found that their life savings would barely buy a bus ticket.

German children use worthless stacks of money as building blocks during the 1923 inflation crisis.

Restructuring the mark

It became obvious that Germany could not escape from the situation without help. Germany, France, and Belgium agreed to end the occupation of the Ruhr, make the debt repayments easier, and set new values on the mark. With loans from the United States and other countries, the German economy settled down and industries began to grow.

Ernest Hemingway visits Germany during the hyperinflation

In September 1922, the writer Ernest Hemingway visited Kehl, a border town in Germany. He watched French people cross the border to eat as much as they could in German cafes, paying almost nothing while the locals could barely afford to eat.

"It is a sight every afternoon to see the mob that storms the German pastry shops and tea places. The Germans make very good pastries. At the present tumbling mark rate, the French can buy them for less than the smallest French coin. The youth of the (French) town of Strasbourg crowd into the German pastry shops to eat themselves sick and gorge on fluffy, cream filled slices of German cake ..."

(FROM *BY-LINE: ERNEST HEMINGWAY* EDITED BY WILLIAM WHITE)

Hungry German children wait to be fed at a street-kitchen in post-war Germany, December 1918.

The Wall Street Crash

After the First World War the US economy flourished, encouraged by low taxes and laws that encouraged industry and prevented strikes. As businesses grew, people invested in them by buying **stocks and shares**. These were traded on the New York Stock Exchange, on Wall Street. During the 1920s, the price of shares rose, as more and more people invested in them. Eventually shares became overpriced, but as long as prices were rising no one minded. Ordinary people took out bank loans to buy shares. They knew that when their shares went up in price they could sell them, pay back the bank loan, and get some profit as well.

The crash

Then, in October 1929, rumours began to spread that dishonest dealing was taking place in the stock market. Share prices were being deliberately pushed up and then suddenly sold. Panic selling began on 24 October as people rushed to get rid of their shares before they lost their value.

On 29 October share prices collapsed completely. The shares that people had bought at a high price were now worth very little.

The aftermath

On 24 October, almost 13 million shares changed hands. Five days later, 15 million shares changed hands at only a few cents each. Huge US companies such as General Motors and General Electric found that everyone wanted to sell their shares at any price, but no one was buying any. Several investors committed suicide by throwing themselves out of the windows of the tall Wall Street buildings. Bus companies advertised bus trips to the street to watch the panic.

People crowd Wall Street, New York, after the stock market crash of October 1929.

Wall Street panic

On Black Tuesday (29 October 1929), the market completely collapsed. A Wall Street security guard describes the sudden panic that broke out in the Stock Exchange:

"[The investors] roared like a lot of lions and tigers. They hollered and screamed, they clawed at each others collars. It was like a bunch of crazy men. Every once in a while, when a major business took another tumble, you'd see some poor devil collapse and fall to the floor."

(FROM THE HERBERT HOOVER PRESIDENTIAL LIBRARY AND MUSEUM, WEST BRANCH, IOWA)

The consequences

Thousands of people who had made huge fortunes on the stock market found that suddenly they had debts that they could never hope to pay back. Ordinary people could not repay their bank loans and lost everything they had, including their homes. Banks that had bought shares with their customers' money went out of business and their customers lost their savings. The employees of banks and investment companies found themselves out of work. Businesses suddenly lost their value and customers as no one had money to buy the goods they made. They closed down and put their employees out of work.

New Yorker Walter Thornton sells his expensive car for just $100 after he lost everything in the stock market crash.

The Depression

People lived in the poor conditions of "Hooverville" camp sites (such as this one in Seattle, United States) while they looked for work in the cities during the Depression.

The Wall Street Crash affected the rest of the world and its consequences lasted for many years. By 1932, US$74 billion had been wiped off the value of United States stocks and shares, three times more money than America had spent on the First World War. Factories shut down as investment stopped and customers disappeared. As more people were thrown out of work, demand for goods fell again, and a spiral of unemployment and business closures began. Even those in work had to take wage cuts of 40–60 per cent. Five thousand banks went out of business, taking their customers's money with them.

The social consequences

It was estimated by 1932 that 34 million people, 28 per cent of the US population, had no income. Food prices fell so low that the cost of transport to the markets was higher than any profits that the farmers could make. People began to suffer the effects of malnutrition while 2 million men and women began to travel around the country looking for any kind of work. Arriving in the cities and unable to find work, thousands of people set up camp sites in city parks. These came to be known as Hoovervilles after the current President Herbert Hoover. Some Americans even **emigrated** to Russia to find work. The United States economic depression remained until the outbreak of the Second World War in 1939, when the demand for weapons gave the economy the boost it needed.

Global depression

The struggling US banks had to demand back the money they had loaned to foreign companies. The German economy, which had relied heavily on United States loans, went into a decline. In the UK, also heavily dependent on United States loans, the economy slowed down. Countries such as China, Chile, Japan, and Malaya – all of which depended on the export of **raw materials** around the world – experienced a slump in demand. The total value of world trade in 1932 was US$992 million compared to US$2998 million in 1929. As other countries in Europe and around the world struggled with their own problems they withdrew their reserves of gold from US banks. This added to the problems of US banks, which depended on gold reserves and the banks began to go out of business even quicker.

People queue for handouts of soup and coffee in New York during the Depression, 1935.

Brother, can you spare a dime?

These are the despairing lyrics of a popular song of the time, supposedly the words spoken by a man begging on the street:

"Once I built a railroad
I made it run
Made it race against time
Once I built a railroad
Now it's done
Brother, can you spare a dime?

Once I built a tower
Up to the sun
Bricks and rivets and lime
Once I built a tower
Now it's done
Brother, can you spare a dime?"

(BY EDGAR "YIP" HARBURG IN 1932)

In the 1920s, a generation of men who had fought in the terrible conditions of the First World War had re-established a normal life in the UK. As the decade was drawing to an end, events in Germany, with the development of **anti-Semitism**, were far from people's minds and no one was ready to face the prospect of another world war. In 1931, Oswald Mosely, an ex-Labour-Party politician, set up the UK equivalent of the Nazis. It had little support, met huge opposition and faded away as British people did not agree with blaming Jews for economic problems.

The Nazis

The global depression of 1929 hit Germany very badly. This was partly responsible for bringing into power a political group that promised a way out of the depression. Adolf Hitler was the leader of this Nazi party. At the time of the stock market crash, the Nazis had the support of only 2.6 per cent of Germans, but this soon grew.

Who was Hitler?

Born in Austria in 1889, Adolf Hitler was an average school pupil. He tried to get into art school in Vienna, but was turned down. He moved to Vienna, living on handouts from his widowed mother and scraping a living by painting postcards. According to his autobiography it was in these years of hardship that he came to hate Jewish people. At the end of the First World War, in which he had fought, Hitler decided to go into politics and discovered a party that would later be called the Nazis. Joining this party, Hitler soon became its leader.

Adolf Hitler leaves Leusberg Prison, Germany, 1 January 1924 (the place where he wrote his autobiography *Mein Kampf*).

Hitler's anti-Semitism

In his autobiography, called *Mein Kampf* (My Struggle), Hitler describes how he came to hate Jewish people while living in Vienna in the early 1900s. He was very poor and all around him he saw wealthy Jewish people who were important figures in art, politics, science, and finance. From this, Hitler took up anti-Semitic ideas, believing that the Jews were a kind of disease that weakened whatever society they moved into.

The beer hall putsch

Hitler blamed the Socialist German government and the Jews for the harsh conditions forced on Germany in the **Treaty of Versailles**. He also blamed them for the economic slump of the early 1920s. In 1923, he and his followers tried to take over the government. While a government minister was making a speech in a large beer hall in Munich, a group of Nazis armed with guns broke into the hall and announced a revolution. The attempt failed and Hitler was arrested and sent to prison. When he was released a year later he found that the Nazi party had become disorganized and that the German economy, helped by United States loans, was improving.

Heinrich Himmler (a senior Nazi party member) waves the flag of the Nazi party prior to the takeover of the Munich beer hall on 7 November 1923.

Hitler gains power

Once released from prison, Hitler began to campaign against the war fines that Germany was forced to pay. He also began to organize Nazi-supporting groups among various professions. In the elections of 1928, however, the Nazis did badly, getting only a tiny fraction of the national vote.

The effects of the Wall Street Crash

The effects of the Wall Street Crash on Germany were immediate:

- US banks called in their loans to German companies
- prices of German stocks and shares began to fall
- banks and manufacturers began to go out of business.

By 1932:

- unemployment had reached 6.5 million
- German industry was working at half its production levels of 1928
- German foreign trade had fallen by two thirds.

Hitler's party was able to use all of this to gain support.

Hitler becomes Chancellor

From 1930 to 1932, as the economic depression worsened, Hitler's party gained more and more support. In elections in July 1932, the Nazis took 37 per cent of the vote. This was still not enough to make them the dominant party in Germany and it was not until 1933 that the Nazis, together with other **extremist** parties, were strong enough to have Hitler named as the German **Chancellor**.

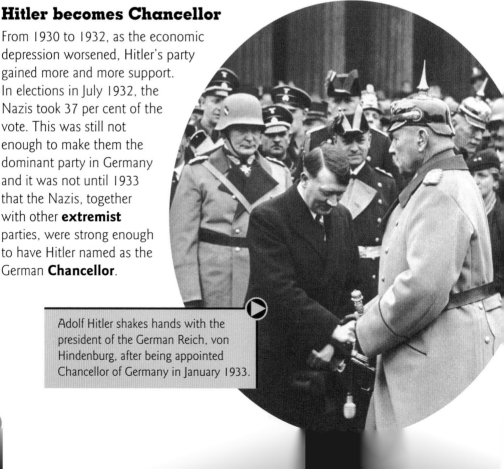

Adolf Hitler shakes hands with the president of the German Reich, von Hindenburg, after being appointed Chancellor of Germany in January 1933.

The Reichstag fire

Hitler was now Chancellor, but he had to put up with members of other parties in government jobs. As new elections were being organised, the Reichstag, the German parliament, caught fire and burned to the ground. Hitler blamed the communists and used the event to pass a law giving him enormous emergency powers and suspending the normal rights of citizens. After the next set of elections in March 1933, when again the Nazis did not get a majority, Hitler forced the Reichstag to pass a law giving all law-making powers to his government. This was the end of **democracy** in Germany and it made Hitler a dictator.

While he was building up the Nazi party Hitler had created a group called the **SA**, or storm troopers. Its members had regularly attacked Jewish businesses and communist groups. Now that Hitler had become Chancellor the storm troopers were a bit of an embarrassment, and in 1934 he had the SA leadership arrested and executed.

The Reichstag is set alight on 27 February 1933. A Dutch communist, Marinus van der Lubbe, was found at the scene by leading Nazis, and was later charged with arson and executed.

The Enabling Law of 1933

In March 1933, Hitler's party again failed to get a majority in the Reichstag, the German parliament. Hitler wanted parliament to pass an **Enabling Law**, however, which would give all law-making powers to his government. When the Reichstag met on 23 March 1933, Hitler surrounded the building with his private armies. The 81 communist MPs had either been arrested or were blocked from entering the building. Inside the building the SA intimidated MPs into voting for the Enabling Law. Everyone knew that to vote against Hitler would be dangerous. The law was passed by 441 votes to 94.

Why was Hitler so popular?

Hitler offered simple solutions to complicated problems:

- he blamed Germany's problems on the Jews, the communists, and the people who had signed the Treaty of Versailles at the end of the First World War
- anti-Semitism (hatred of Jews) had been a problem in Europe for hundreds of years. Jews had been wrongly blamed for other problems in many countries. Hitler made use of that hatred
- Hitler was also able to exploit the fear of communism. Middle-class Germans had seen the communist revolutions that had gone on in other countries and were afraid of the communist party in Germany
- lastly, Hitler's ideas were all about German nationalism and this appealed to the simple pride of the German people. They had been unfairly treated by the terms of the Treaty of Versailles and Hitler offered them self-respect once more.

Hitler was popular with all ages. Here, thousands of Hitler Youth members salute the dictator during the Nuremberg Nazi Party Congress, 19 September 1938.

The Nazi manifesto

In 1920, the Nazi party drew up a list of their policies. These are a few of them:

1. Seize land outside Germany to provide food and new homes for Germans
2. German citizenship is only to be allowed for German people, i.e. German Jews cannot be German citizens
3. Any further immigration of non-Germans is to be halted and all people who entered Germany after 1914 are to be forced to leave Germany immediately
4. All moneylenders and people who exploit Germans are to be punished by death without regard to religion or race.

(FROM A QUOTATION IN *STUDYING THE HOLOCAUST* BY RONNIE LANDAU)

Who supported Hitler?

Hitler's ideas appealed to different groups of people for different reasons:

- young people were attracted to his ideas because they were simple and appealing. Hitler had started a Hitler Youth movement and when these people became old enough they voted for him.
- farmers were attracted to Hitler's ideas because the Nazis promised an end to low farm prices. Also, many rural areas of Germany were traditionally anti-Semitic.
- lots of ordinary people who had lost their jobs believed Hitler's promises of new jobs.
- all the people who had grown tired of weak governments since the end of the war saw a strong leader in Hitler.
- wealthy people were afraid that a communist government in Germany would take away their wealth and property, so they wanted anything but this.

Germany's Jews

About 550,000 Jews lived in Germany in 1930, about 1 per cent of the total population. They came from all classes and did all kinds of jobs from manual work to being artists, industrialists, and bankers. They were well integrated into German life and considered themselves Germans. Thousands of Jews joined the German army in 1914 and, for the first time in history, fought against French or British Jews in the Allied armies. They were equally hit by Germany's economic collapse, but suffered at the same time from the increasing verbal and physical attacks of the SA and other racists. Most German Jews were loyal, hardworking citizens, hoping desperately that when the economic problems improved the racism would stop.

WORLD IN TROUBLE

In 1933, the UK gave little thought to what was happening in Germany. Most people thought that Hitler's party would soon be replaced by a more moderate government. Unknown to the UK, though, Hitler was secretly building up Germany's armies and weapons, and in 1936, he moved German troops into the Rhineland, an area of Germany. This had been forbidden by the Treaty of Versailles. The UK, France, and Italy met to discuss the threat and decided that the best thing to do was to tolerate it for the time being.

Dictatorship in Italy

In 1922, Mussolini, at age 39, became the youngest prime minister in Italian history. For a few years he made a decent job of ruling the country, improving the economy and the lives of ordinary people. People were guaranteed a day off on Sundays and there was a system of social security in case of unemployment or illness. Sports facilities and theatres were built. World leaders admired him and many Italians considered him a genius. These improvements, however, came at a price.

The cost of fascism

The cost of fascism was that other political parties were banned and those who opposed the government were forced to leave the country or murdered. The Italian parliament, the group of elected men whose job it had been to pass new laws, became powerless. Also, only wealthy people could vote. This reduced the number of people who could vote from 10 million to 3 million. All local elections were abolished. Newspapers, radio, films, theatres, and schools were censored.

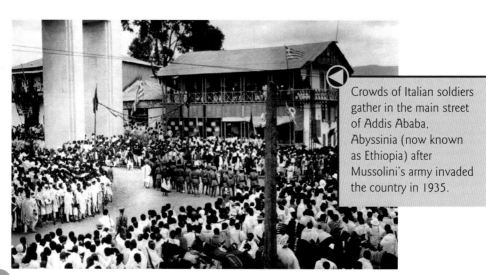

Crowds of Italian soldiers gather in the main street of Addis Ababa, Abyssinia (now known as Ethiopia) after Mussolini's army invaded the country in 1935.

Building an empire

Italy was improving, but it needed raw materials for its industries and new land for Italian farmers. Mussolini saw the African country of Abyssinia (now Ethiopia) as a good target for expansion. The invasion, beginning in 1935, took almost a year. France and the UK chose not to interfere. The final success of Mussolini's invasion made Hitler realize that the Allies were not ready for another war. Hitler and Mussolini became allies and Hitler set about breaking the terms of the Treaty of Versailles, confident that no one would stop him.

Mussolini's dream of empire

"The aim we have in mind is the development and exploitation of the resources of Africa. Italy is in a position to do this. We intend to make clear that those countries who arrived ahead of us [e.g. the UK and France] should not try to block the spiritual, political, and economic expansion of fascist Italy."

(FROM A SPEECH GIVEN IN ROME IN MARCH 1934. QUOTED IN THE ORIGINS OF THE SECOND WORLD WAR BY R. J. OVERY)

Benito Mussolini welcomes Adolf Hitler to Italy as their political friendship grows, 14 June 1934.

Stalin in Russia

In Russia, peasants were suffering terribly because the grain they were producing was being seized and used to feed the army. Lenin, the leader of Russia and one of the men who had led the Russian revolution, began to solve these problems. In 1921, he introduced a new policy of allowing the peasants to make some profit from the food they produced, encouraging them to produce even more. The economy began to recover, industry was modernized, and Russian citizens were better off than they had been since the start of the First World War. In 1922, Lenin created the **USSR**, joining Russia with neighbouring countries to create one huge country.

In 1924, Lenin died, leaving the revolution half completed. His death created a power struggle between two other men – Leon Trotsky, one of the original leaders of the revolution, and Joseph Stalin. Stalin won and by 1928 he was virtual dictator.

Members of Lenin's government carry his coffin to the Labor Temple in Moscow, USSR, 30 January 1924.

Lenin

Vladimir Ilyich Lenin was the son of a school inspector and gained a degree in law from St Petersburg University. He was outspoken about the need for social and political reform in Russia, so he was imprisoned by the Tsar in 1895 and then sent to Siberia. In 1900, Lenin was forced to leave Russia to live abroad. In 1917, he returned to Russia and gave the Russian revolutionaries the ideas they needed to carry out their revolution. By October 1917, Lenin was the leader of the revolution. By 1922, however, his health was in decline and 2 years later he died, aged 54.

Stalin's changes

Stalin inherited the problem Lenin had encountered, which was that the USSR was basically a country where most people were poor farmers. The USSR needed to become an industrial country very quickly in order to provide for all of its people. Stalin chose to tackle this problem head on and brought about violent changes to agriculture. This was called **collectivisation**. Farming was taken over by the government, who joined up lots of small farms into really huge ones. There was strong resistance by wealthier peasants whose profits from farming would completely disappear. These wealthier peasants, called kulaks, a nickname meaning "fat ones", reacted by killing their cattle and wasting their crops. This led to terrible famines in 1932–1933, in which

This is a poster of Joseph Stalin in his military uniform.

5 million peasants died of starvation and 10 million of those that refused to join the collective farms were driven away or killed. Stalin's wife killed herself in protest.

Totalitarianism

Many people in the communist party believed that, although Stalin's reforms were the right thing to do, they were being done too quickly, especially the collectivisation of farms. Some areas of the country began calling for independence. However, in 1934, Stalin began wiping out all his political opponents in a series of **purges**. Most of the leaders of the 1917 revolution were murdered and several million ordinary people were sent off to labour camps called "**gulags**". Artists and musicians were forced into producing work that celebrated the growth of the USSR.

The mid 1930s

In the mid 1930s, life in many countries looked bleak. There was civil war in China, as two parties fought for control of the country. By 1936, there was civil war in Spain between a new government and those that had been replaced. Western Europe and beyond was caught up in an economic depression. Germany and Italy were both building-up arms and threatening their neighbours with invasion. Other countries such as the UK and the United States were not yet ready to begin another war. In the United States, the Great Depression still had the country in its grip and nobody wanted to get involved in European matters.

The new deal

In the United States, a new president, Franklin D. Roosevelt, took up office in 1933. His first task was to restore the US people's confidence in the economy. Roosevelt was a great communicator. He gave radio talks, which he called "fireside chats". These made people confident he could pull the United States out of the Depression.

▲ Franklin D. Roosevelt makes his first address as 32nd president of the United States, 1933.

Roosevelt's first measure was to restore confidence in the banking system. The government guaranteed that people who put their money into the bank would not lose their savings if another financial crisis happened. Then, in 1933, the government gave compensation to farmers who produced less food. This raised the price of farm products so that farmers could make a living wage. He provided work for unemployed youths in conservation projects, which gave them an income and improved the countryside.

Most importantly he introduced the Public Works Administration. This set up government projects such as building dams, roads, hospitals, and schools. As men were given jobs, the money they earned stimulated the economy and so factories reopened, shops sold more goods, and more people found jobs. Old age pensions and unemployment pay were introduced. Within a few years the United States had begun to rise out of the Depression.

Military rule in Japan

In Japan, the government became very unpopular because the Great Depression had created economic problems there. The army gradually took power and was determined to create a strong Japan that would not be dependent on the West. This meant expanding into other countries such as China. This would certainly lead to trouble between Japan and countries that were already operating out of China, especially the United States.

Civil war in China

In China by the mid 1930s, with a civil war raging for control of the country, life was extremely hard. One of Mao Zedong's soldiers recalls the suffering:

"The [enemy] troops burned down all the houses in the surrounding area, seized all the food there and then **blockaded** us. We had no shelter, no lights and no salt. We were sick and half starved. The peasants were no better off and we would not touch what little they had. But the peasants encouraged us. They dug up from the ground the grain, which they had hidden from the troops and gave it to us, and they ate potatoes and wild roots."

(FROM RED STAR OVER CHINA BY EDGAR SNOW)

Chinese soldiers prepare to fight during the civil war of the mid 1930s.

TIMELINE

1919
The IRA begins its war of
   independence in Ireland
The zip fastener arrives in the UK
In the UK women over age 30 are
   given the vote
British troops open fire on a meeting
   in Amritsar, India

1920
Charlie Chaplin makes his first full
   length film *The Kid*
Prohibition in the United States.
   Al Capone arrives in Chicago
US women get the vote

1921
Unemployment rises all over Europe
Mutiny in Kronstadt, Russia, is
   suppressed
Widespread famine in Russia
German war reparations fixed at
   £6.6 billion
The first birth control clinic is
   opened in the UK
Scientists discover insulin
Albert Einstein is awarded the Nobel
   Prize for Physics
The Anglo Irish treaty is signed,
   dividing Ireland into two countries

1922
Mussolini takes power in Italy
In India, Gandhi is sent to prison
Civil war breaks out in Ireland
Ulysses is published in Paris
Tutankhamen's tomb is opened
   in Egypt
Public broadcasting officially begins
   in the UK

1923
Civil war in Ireland comes to an end
The mark collapses in Germany
Hitler attempts to take power
   in Germany
Margaret Sanger opens the first US
   birth control clinic in New York

1924
Death of Vladimir Ilyich Lenin
Passenger airlines begin regular
   services between European cities

1925
Hitler publishes *Mein Kampf*
The Charleston dance craze reaches
   Europe
Fashionable women's hemlines
   reach their knees
Louis Armstrong forms his band the
   Hot Fives
An exhibition in France gives its
   name to the new kind of
   decoration: Art Deco

1926

General Strike in the UK
Rudolph Valentino dies
The UK national grid is established,
 bringing electricity to a fifth of
 UK homes. BBC broadcasts reach
 85 per cent of the UK

1927

Charles Lindbergh makes the first
 solo flight across the Atlantic
The first films to incorporate a
 soundtrack are made
Nationalists take power in China

1928

Herbert Hoover becomes president
 of the United States
Stalin consolidates his power in
 Russia. Collective farms established
The first Mickey Mouse cartoon
 is made
Alexander Fleming discovers
 penicillin
The first television pictures are
 transmitted across the Atlantic

1929

Indians begin a campaign to boycott
 UK goods
The Wall Street Crash
The German airship Graf Zeppelin
 makes a round-the-world trip
The St Valentine's Day Massacre
The Depression begins

1930

The Chrysler Building is opened
Indians begin a boycott of the salt tax

1931

The Empire State Building is opened

1932

World Trade hits a new low
In the UK, Oswald Mosely forms
 the British Union of Fascists

1933

Famine in Russia
Gandhi begins a hunger strike
 in India
Hitler takes power in Germany
Prohibition comes to an end in
 the United States
Roosevelt becomes president in the
 United States and created the
 New Deal

1934

The Long March in China
The Night of the Long Knives
 in Germany

1936

Civil war in Spain

51

CDs

This Sceptered Isle Volume 2 1919–1939 (BBC Audiobooks, 1998)
Eyewitness: The 1920s (BBC Audiobooks, 2004)
Eyewitness: The 1930s (BBC Audiobooks, 2004)

Books

Artists in Profile: Surrealists, Linda Bolton (Heinemann Library, 2002)
Digging Deeper: The Twentieth Century World, Alan Brooks-Tyreman, Jane Shuter, and Kate Smith (Heinemann Library, 2000)
In World History: Mahatma Gandhi and India's Independence in World History, Ann Malaspina (Enslow, 2000)
Jam! The Story of Jazz Music, Jeanne Lee (Rosen, 1999)
Living Through History: The Twentieth Century World, Nigel Kelly (Heinemann Library, 1998)
The 1920s (Fashion Sourcebooks), John Peacock (Thames and Hudson, 1997)
The New Deal and the Great Depression in American History, Lisa A. Noble (Enslow, 2002)
Turning Points in History: The Long March, Tony Allen (Heinemann Library, 2002)
20th Century Media: 1920s and 1930s: Entertainment for the People, Steve Parker (Heinemann Library, 2002)
20th Century Music: 20s & 30s. Between the Wars, Jackie Gaff (Heinemann Library, 2001)
20th Century Science & Technology: 1920–1940: Science for the People, Steve Parker (Heinemann Library, 2001)

Websites

http://en.wikipedia.org/wiki/1900s
This encyclopedia has sections on the 1920s and the 1930s.

http://www.geocities.com/historygateway/1900.html
Find interesting sites relevant to the history of women in the UK.

http://kclibrary.nhmccd.edu/decades.html
A history site dedicated to US cultural history on a decade-by-decade basis.

Disclaimer

All the internet addresses (URLs) given in this book were valid at the time of going to press. However, due to the dynamic nature of the Internet, some addresses may have changed, or sites may have ceased to exist since publication. While the author and publishers regret any inconvenience this may cause readers, no responsibility for any such changes can be accepted by either the author or the publishers.

the early 1920s to mid 1930s

Books and literature	• *The Voyages of Doctor Dolittle* by Hugh Lofting (1923) • *The Waste Land* by T. S. Eliot (1922) • *Goodbye, Mr Chips* by James Hilton (1934)
Education	• The first 100 women are admitted to study full university degrees at Oxford University, UK, in 1920
Fads and fashions	• The Miss America contest begins in Atlantic City, New Jersey, United States. Margaret Gorman, aged 16 years, is the first winner. • The board game Monopoly is introduced in 1935. 20,000 sets are sold in one week
Historic events	• The ninth major planet, Pluto, is discovered in 1930 • Scotland's Alexander Fleming discovers penicillin on a dish of mould in his laboratory, 1928
Music, film, and theatre	• The first Oscars are given in 1927. *Wings* is the first winning movie. • The British Broadcasting Corporation (BBC) is formed in 1922 • US Congress designates "The Star Spangled Banner" to be the United States' national anthem (1931)
People	• Harry Houdini, the great escape artist, dies in 1926 from appendicitis • British actor Peter Ustinov is born in 1921

abstract not a recognizable picture of something

Allies countries at war against Germany, Austria-Hungary, Turkey, and Bulgaria in the First World War

anarchist someone who believes society can be organized without the need for any form of control

anglepoise type of free-standing light that can be angled into different positions

antibiotic substance made from living bacteria that can cure some illnesses

anti-Semitism hatred of Jewish people

birth control preventing pregnancy

blockade methods used to prevent something happening

boycott refusing to have anything to do with a person or a group as a form of protest

British Empire countries that Britain had invaded and taken control of

cabaret entertainment provided at a place where food is also served

censored when a newspaper, radio, or television is unable to print news because the government prohibits it

Chancellor head of government in Germany, like a prime minister

civil war a war taking place within a country, not against a country

collectivisation bringing farms together to work as one large unit

communist person who believes in organizing a socialist society where the government controls many aspects of life

conscious fully aware of, not hidden

contraceptive sort of birth control

corset close-fitting underwear that holds in the body tightly

culture ways in which a society or a group expresses itself

democracy government where the people of the country choose their leaders by voting for them

Depression period following the Wall Street Crash when industries all over the world went out of business and millions of people were unemployed

diabetes disease that prevents the body from absorbing sugar

dictator ruler with all the power

economic depression period of unemployment when most people spend less

economy matters to do with money

empire control of other countries by a dominant power

emigrate to leave one's country in order to find work in another country

Enabling Law law passed in the German parliament that gave Hitler's party the power to pass whatever new laws it wanted

enamelled when a hard shiny surface is put on to metal or some other substance

extremist person or political group that holds very strong views

fascism system of government that does not allow people to disagree

gramophone machine for playing recorded music (no longer in use)

guerrilla war form of fighting against larger and more powerful forces which avoids an open battle

gulags harsh labour camps

hunger strike refusing to take food or water as a form of protest

immigration movement of people into a country from another country

inflation when prices are rising very rapidly

insulin substance produced by the human body which enables it to absorb sugar

jazz type of music, usually without words, that began in the United States in the 20th century

mass production when something is made in factories by machines in large numbers rather than one at a time by an individual

modernist new and untraditional forms of art

mutiny open rebellion against authority

nationalist someone with a strong belief in the value of the nation to which they belong

parliament place where politicians make decisions and pass laws

patriotic very loyal to one's country

peasant poor person who works on the land

penicillin drug used to treat various diseases

Perspex tough, transparent plastic that is lighter than glass and does not splinter

prohibition law banning the distribution and consumption of alcohol

protection rackets gangs of criminals who, in exchange for money, do not destroy your business

Protestant set of Christian beliefs belonging to the Protestant church

purge removal of your opponents within a group

raw materials basic products, like iron or oil for example, used in the manufacture of other products

realism in art, making things look like they do in real life

rebellion rising up against an authority

SA storm troopers, Hitler's private army

shingles illness of the skin or the name of a haircut

socialist person who believes in equality and a fairer distribution of wealth

social security government system of payments designed to help the poor

speakeasy illegal drinking parlour

stocks and shares certificates to say that someone owns a part of a company

strike refusing to work in order to obtain better pay or working conditions

territory land belonging to someone

trade union organization formed by workers to protect their interests

treaty agreement between two groups or governments

Treaty of Versailles peace agreement made after the First World War

tuberculosis disease of the body that can kill people, often shortened to TB

USSR Union of Soviet Socialist Republics, a communist state dominated by Russia that disbanded in 1991